The Buffalo
and
the River

BLUE CRAB PRESS
ANNAPOLIS, MARYLAND

Printed in the
United States of America
First Printing 1990
ISBN 0-9627726-0-7

Library of Congress Catalog Number 90-84005
Copyright 1990 by Blue Crab Press
3 Church Circle, Suite 140
Annapolis, Maryland 21401

3 Church Circle, Suite 140
Annapolis, Maryland 21401

The Buffalo
and
the River

Text by Mick Blackistone
Illustrated by Jennifer Heyd Wharton

*"Man did not weave
the web of life,
he is merely a
strand in it.
Whatever he does
to the web, he does
to himself."*
—Chief Seattle

From the time he was four years old,
Peter was attracted to the river. He enjoyed
watching it in the morning when the
fishermen would leave home to go
out in their boats to catch clams, oysters,
crabs or fish—depending on the season.
He dreamed of going out on the river,
too, and he often hoped that one day
he would get a boat of his own.

Finally, when he was at the end of the fifth grade, Peter's big day came. His parents gave him a small sailboat for his eleventh birthday. And every morning and afternoon, when school was out for summer vacation, he went out on the river to sail his new boat.

It never mattered whether he was sailing as fast as he could with the wind coming from behind pushing him faster and faster, or, meandering aimlessly, slowly exploring the quiet coves, when there was no wind to push him with any speed.

He would always remember, when alone as a silent explorer, what his father had said when he received his boat.

"Practice safe boating," his father said. "Having a boat is a big responsibility and you must be careful even when you are out on the river having a lot of fun. Wear your life jacket, watch out for other boats, and never throw any trash in the water. The river and the Bay are yours to use but remember, it belongs to everyone, especially to the wildlife that live above, beside, and in the water."

"If we are safe boaters and also take care of the water, we can all enjoy it for a long time," his father said many times. And Peter promised that he would remember all the things his father told him.

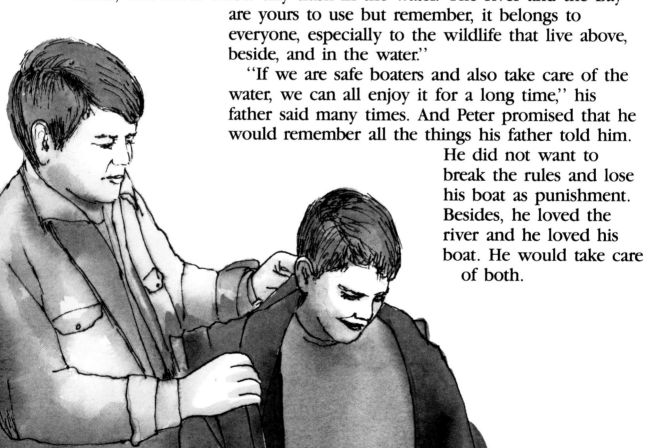

He did not want to break the rules and lose his boat as punishment. Besides, he loved the river and he loved his boat. He would take care of both.

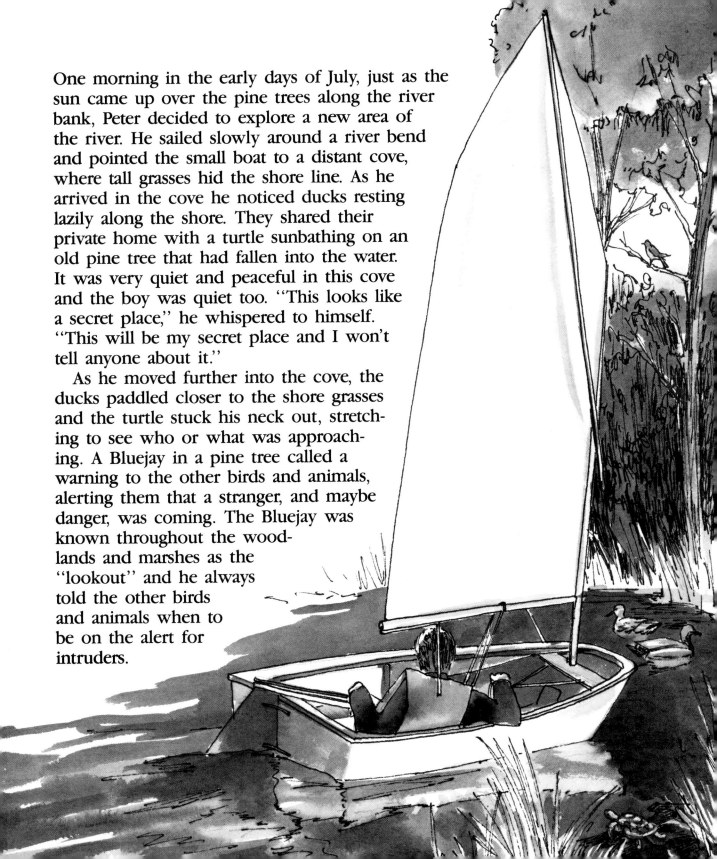

One morning in the early days of July, just as the sun came up over the pine trees along the river bank, Peter decided to explore a new area of the river. He sailed slowly around a river bend and pointed the small boat to a distant cove, where tall grasses hid the shore line. As he arrived in the cove he noticed ducks resting lazily along the shore. They shared their private home with a turtle sunbathing on an old pine tree that had fallen into the water. It was very quiet and peaceful in this cove and the boy was quiet too. "This looks like a secret place," he whispered to himself. "This will be my secret place and I won't tell anyone about it."

As he moved further into the cove, the ducks paddled closer to the shore grasses and the turtle stuck his neck out, stretching to see who or what was approaching. A Bluejay in a pine tree called a warning to the other birds and animals, alerting them that a stranger, and maybe danger, was coming. The Bluejay was known throughout the woodlands and marshes as the "lookout" and he always told the other birds and animals when to be on the alert for intruders.

Slowly searching and inspecting the marsh grass and trees as carefully as he could, Peter was determined to see everything in and around his new "secret place."

Suddenly, as he looked beyond a small patch of wetland, he spotted an old wooden cottage hidden by tall grass and scrub pine trees. It was not painted and, even though it was a bright summer morning, a small stream of smoke came from a rusty pipe chimney.

"Someone must live there," he whispered to himself. "But what do they do there and who could it be?"

Moving closer to the grass thicket, his eyes spotted a narrow path which led from the water's edge to the base of the worn porch steps. The porch was small but there appeared to be an old rocking chair, some wooden crates and other things scattered around. Fish nets hung from the rear wall and a weathered rowboat leaned against the side of the cottage.

As Peter sat silently in his sailboat straining his eyes to see even more, he was suddenly shocked to see the front door begin to open. Nervously he moved into the grass and watched as an old man wearing faded coveralls and a bright red shirt moved slowly towards the rocking chair. As he came into clear view, Peter could see that he wore a blue bandana around his forehead. He had snow-white hair which was tied in a ponytail that fell halfway down his back. The man moved slowly, and even though he was slightly bent, he moved with great determination and ease. Upon reaching the chair, the old man sat, folded his hands on his lap and stared through the scrubby trees, across the marsh grass, over the river toward the rising sun.

As the old man stared across the cove, Peter stared at him. Neither moved for the longest period of time. The ducks had left for distant parts of the cove and the turtle had long since fallen off the old pine tree into the warm water.

Finally, Peter thought it would be a good idea to leave, slowly and quietly, while the old man was in his chair.

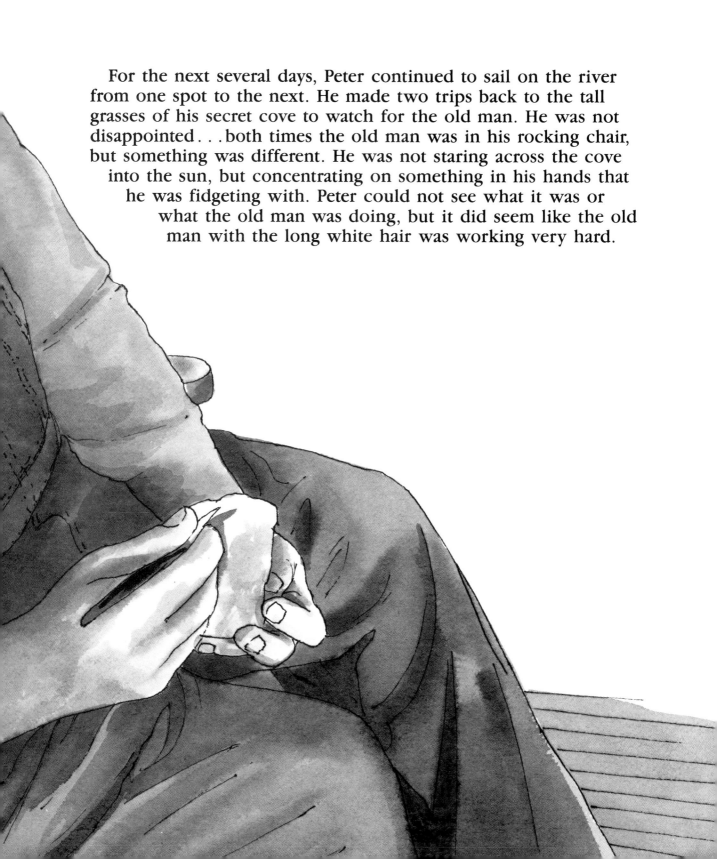

For the next several days, Peter continued to sail on the river from one spot to the next. He made two trips back to the tall grasses of his secret cove to watch for the old man. He was not disappointed. . .both times the old man was in his rocking chair, but something was different. He was not staring across the cove into the sun, but concentrating on something in his hands that he was fidgeting with. Peter could not see what it was or what the old man was doing, but it did seem like the old man with the long white hair was working very hard.

One morning, a week or so later, as Peter got up from bed he noticed that the wind was blowing hard and there were grey clouds in the sky. His father had taught him an old saying among boaters: "When in doubt, don't go out," which meant when you were not sure about good weather stay home and do not use your boat. So today, his plans would include a new expedition: riding his bicycle to the old cottage to spy on the old man.

"Where are you going this early in the morning?" his mother asked as he walked to the door. "With the wind blowing like this, that boat is to stay tied to the dock."

"I know, Mom. I'm riding my bike for a while. I'm going exploring, but I'll be back by lunch time," he responded. He certainly was not going to mention the old man or his cottage back in the wetland by the cove. This was his secret and he wanted to investigate without his mother or father knowing anything about it.

Moments later, he was riding his bicycle down the road to look for a driveway that might lead to the old cottage and the cove off the big river. He rode from his house to where the road was lined with trees and scrub brush. There were no houses anywhere along this stretch of road. Much of the land was low and covered with brackish water.

Pedaling slowly along, he finally spotted a clearing in the trees and brush which was barely wide enough for a car to get through. It was not really a driveway, rather, a long path which wandered back through the trees.

He paused at the path and took a deep breath. He was scared to go forward, not knowing what to expect should he actually meet the old man. Straddling his bicycle he stared at the path, now in shadows, with streaks of sunlight filtering through the branches of the taller trees.

"Oh well," he said to himself gathering courage, "It's now or never." Cautiously, he approached the first curve which lead to the thickest part of the woods. The path was raised above the rest of the landscape, and small areas of water covered many of the tree trunks on either side of the path.

Further ahead he saw thin wisps of smoke rising above the trees and his heart seemed to beat faster and faster. The cottage was only a short distance away. He decided that it would be safer to leave his bicycle and walk the remaining distance to the old man's cottage. Peter knew that if he had to, he could run back to the bicycle and be well on his way before the old man could catch him.

Walking as quietly and cautiously as he could, he moved toward the rising smoke. He could see the old ramshackle cottage and a corner of the porch that faced the cove and the big river beyond.

Approaching the cottage, he did not hear or see any sign of the old man. There was a faded blue pick-up truck parked next to the cottage. Beside the truck were more torn fishing nets piled high beside a rowboat. Neither the truck, boat, nor the fishing nets looked in very good shape. Peter crept silently between the truck and the cottage. He thought the old man might be in his rocking chair and that on this visit maybe all he should do is take a quick look around the corner of the porch, get back to his bicycle, and ride away as fast as he could.

Finally when he was standing right next to the cottage, he was surprised to hear a voice call out, "Do not be afraid, you are welcome here." Peter did not move. He had not even looked around the corner to see the old man and yet the old man knew he was there! "Do not be afraid, show yourself. You are welcome here," the voice said again.

Peter stepped from the side of the house and stood by the corner of the porch. Seated in the rocking chair was the old man in his bright red shirt and faded blue coveralls. He stared out across the cove and did not move. "Come forward. You are a welcomed visitor to my home," the old man said softly.

"But, how did you know I was here?" Peter asked. "I thought I was very quiet."

"Yes, I suppose you were," said the old man. "But I knew you were here when you began walking toward me from the tree line behind the house. The Bluejay told me. I wondered how long it would be before you came. It was only a couple of days ago that you were in the marsh grass aboard your boat."

"You knew I was there, too!" Peter exclaimed.

"Yes. But it doesn't matter. The important thing is that you are here to receive your gift."

"My gift? But I haven't done anything to receive a gift, and it isn't my birthday."

"Yes, you have done an important thing," the old man said softly. "You followed your heart and made a journey. And perhaps on this day you have found something you did not even know you were looking for. Come, sit beside me."

The old man continued to gaze out over the cove to the big river. He sat perfectly still as Peter began to step on the porch and move slowly toward a wooden crate that was next to the rocking chair.

As Peter nervously sat down, the old man finally turned and looked directly into his eyes. The old man's skin was deeply tanned and there were many wrinkles coming from the corner of his eyes. His eyes were clear and blue.

He extended his hand to Peter, who shook it as he had done with his father's friends when they came to visit. The old man's grasp was firm, and the boy felt at ease clutching it briefly. "What do people call you?" the old man asked.

"Peter," said the boy.

"Peter is a good name. My name is John," said the old man.

With his other hand he slowly revealed a blue bandanna similar to the one tied around his head. He leaned forward and handed the bandanna to Peter.

"Thank you," Peter said in a puzzled tone as he began to unwrap the cloth to see what was inside. The cloth revealed a wooden buffalo carved from a lightly colored piece of wood. It was almost eight inches long and stood about six inches high.

"This is what you were working on when I saw you from the cove!" Peter exclaimed. "You were carving this buffalo out of a piece of wood with a knife. But I don't understand why you would give me this buffalo. What does it mean?"

The old man sat back in his rocking chair, folded his weathered hands in his lap, and stared out across the cove to the big river. He began to speak softly.

"Peter, I am a Native American, an Indian, and a descendant of the Piscataway tribe. My grandfathers were born along the river which stretches before your eyes. I, too, was born by the river many years ago. As a young boy there were many fish, clams and oysters to feed us and we had plenty to eat."

"But come with me." The old Indian said. "My skiff is at the water's edge. We can talk there."

Peter stood and followed the old man to a small clearing in the marsh grass. There, beached in the grass was an old wooden rowing boat. Years of sitting unprotected from sun, rain and cold had left the boat gray. The white paint which once covered its hull had long since chipped away.

As they climbed aboard, the old man handed Peter a life jacket to put on as he put a pair of oars in their locks. He told Peter to make himself comfortable. Although Peter felt nervous, he was, nevertheless, anxious to hear what the old man had to say as they slowly moved out into the cove.

"At the time of my grandfathers, there were also Indian brothers on the Great Plains stretching from the Mississippi River west to the setting sun. They did not have fish, clams or oysters to feed them. Instead, they had many buffalo. Do you know that at the time of my father, over one hundred years ago, there were about 60 million buffalo roaming the Great Plains. There were so many buffalo that if you flew over them like a hawk, it would have looked like a great brown blanket covering the ground. They were as plentiful to the Plains Indians as fish, clams and oysters were to my people living here on the big river. Then the white men from the east and Europe began moving west. They began to hunt and kill the buffalo in great numbers. The 60 million soon disappeared to almost zero. The buffalo were almost extinct! And this was a big reason for many of the problems between the Indians and the white men. The killing of the buffalo meant a loss of food, clothing and trading power for the Indian people. It also meant the loss of their freedom and a way of life."

"But there are some buffalo now," Peter interrupted. "I have seen them in the zoo, on television and at Yellowstone National Park when we went there on vacation."

"That is right, Peter. There are some buffalo now, but only because a few ranchers and conservationists were determined to save them by having the government protect them and place them in areas where they could not be hunted."

"But I still don't understand what the buffalo and your Indian ancestors have to do with me," Peter said.

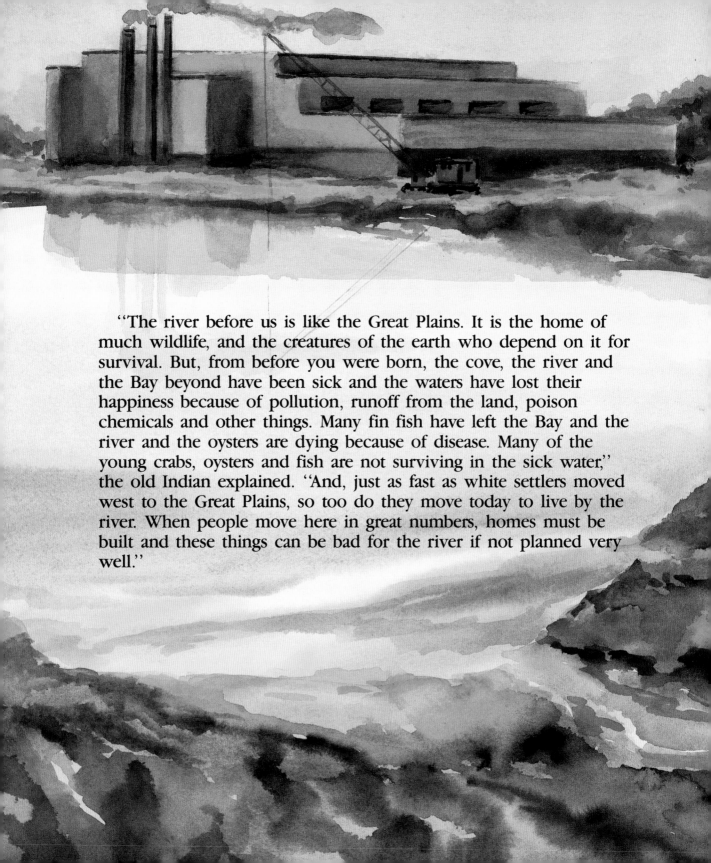

"The river before us is like the Great Plains. It is the home of much wildlife, and the creatures of the earth who depend on it for survival. But, from before you were born, the cove, the river and the Bay beyond have been sick and the waters have lost their happiness because of pollution, runoff from the land, poison chemicals and other things. Many fin fish have left the Bay and the river and the oysters are dying because of disease. Many of the young crabs, oysters and fish are not surviving in the sick water," the old Indian explained. "And, just as fast as white settlers moved west to the Great Plains, so too do they move today to live by the river. When people move here in great numbers, homes must be built and these things can be bad for the river if not planned very well."

"Have you heard your father or mother talk about the rockfish or striped bass, a very famous fish from our river?" the old man asked.

"Sure," said Peter, "everybody knows about the rockfish. Even people in England and France."

"That's right," responded the old man, "but now the people are sad because they cannot eat much rockfish from the big river. You see, when the waters were clean and healthy, the great rockfish came down the ocean coast in large numbers into the Bay and up the rivers to spawn, or lay their eggs. There were millions of rockfish and fishermen caught them for everyone to eat. Then pollution started to make the water sick and very unhealthy for the rockfish and their young. The young died and after a few years, the rockfish were not coming to the river and other areas to lay their eggs. The rockfish were, like the buffalo, leaving old homes. We did not see them very much and the people were sad."

"So what happened?" asked Peter. "Did most of them die like the buffalo?"

"Well, many were dying and others were simply not coming here," said the old man.

"So the people of the bays and rivers, the fishermen and the government workers agreed to clean up the waters and they also agreed not to catch any more rockfish so that they too would come back to the bays and rivers like the buffalo to the Great Plains."

"Now after several winters of no fishing for rockfish and people cleaning up the water where the fish lay their eggs, the rockfish are coming back to us. Now we are able to catch and eat them again," the old man said.

"That's good," said Peter. "The rockfish came back just like the buffalo because poeple cared and worked really hard to make their homes better for them."

"This is true," said the old man. "But we must still worry about our other fish: the perch, herring, shad, bluefish, and our crabs, clams and oysters."

As the old man rowed further out into the river he suddenly sensed a change in the wind and his years of living near the river told him they were about to have a change in the weather. It had been cloudy early in the morning and he knew that storms came very quickly. It would be best to row for the safety of the cove. But it was too late. Without warning dark clouds appeared, the wind began to blow again and the river which was calm minutes before was now churning with rolling waves.

"Peter, this does not look good. Tighten your life jacket then hold these oars while I secure mine. This old boat may not have the strength to hold up in a summer storm. Sit on the floor while I try to reach the cove."

Peter sat in the stern of the small boat. With one hand he held on to his buffalo and with the other to the side of the boat as the waves rocked him from side to side. He was scared now as he watched the old man row as fast as he could. "This is nature's way of reminding us that we, as people, are not always in control and that we must respect what nature shows us," the old man yelled as the storm grew more violent and rain began to fall very hard. "When we think that we are in control and that we can play games with nature we are reminded that it has been here for all time and we are merely passing through," the old man said.

"What do you mean?" Peter screamed as he huddled from the rain and wondered in confusion about what the old man was telling him.

Suddenly, before the old man could answer Peter's question, a mighty roll of the waves hit the small rowboat and it flipped over. Peter, clutching his buffalo, was kicking wildly as he hit the water and his only thoughts were to breath and to find the old man.

As he kicked and kicked his body began to feel weak and when his head came through the surface rain beat into his eyes. A wave broke over his head causing him to choke and cough violently. He shook his head and tried desperately to call for John but another wave crashed into his face and he began choking again. The same thing happened each time Peter came to the surface: a wave would force water into his mouth and nose and he would choke. His legs were getting very tired. He tried swimming but it was no use.

Suddenly everything went black and Peter felt as if he were floating. And then everything was calm and very quiet. Peter, strangely enough, was no longer in the water but was suddenly riding on the back of his carved buffalo which had come alive and was carrying him through the sky!

"Hey, where are we going? What's going on? I don't want to do this. I want to go home," Peter yelled out loud. "I'm scared. You're not supposed to be big and alive and flying! You were carved out of wood by the old Indian, John. Please take me home!"

But the giant buffalo moved on through swirling clouds of pink and yellow.

Finally, the clouds opened. Peter looked down and saw the Great Plains. The land went on for miles and there were no cities or roads. All at once they passed over a large herd of buffalo. Hundreds of buffalo, but something was wrong. As they flew closer Peter could see more clearly. Men were shooting the buffalo and they had nowhere to run. The buffalo were being killed.

"Hey, stop shooting! Stop shooting," Peter yelled. "Don't kill all the buffalo. There won't be any left if you kill them. Stop shooting!" Tears fell from his eyes as Peter watched as all the buffalo slowly disappeared before his eyes. "Why didn't they listen?" he cried as the Great Plains faded behind more pink and yellow clouds.

Moments later there was another clearing beneath the clouds. But this time the river lay below and the giant buffalo took Peter over the flowing waters. "Are you taking me home?" he asked shyly. "I recognize the river and I can see the big city where my dad works."

But the great buffalo did not take him home. Instead it took him over the fishermen working on the water. They were pulling up their nets but they were empty because there were no fish. And other fishermen looked sad as they returned home with only a few clams aboard their boats.

"The men don't look happy," Peter said to the giant buffalo as the creature turned to fly up river toward the city. Minutes later the giant buffalo paused in mid-air and Peter could see the land stretching all around the river where he lived. He saw a factory pouring poisonous chemicals into the river; he saw a farmer spreading fertilizer on his land and much of it going into a creek which flowed into the big river; he saw a bulldozer pushing dirt into a creek to clear land to build new houses; he saw some people in the town throwing trash from their car windows, and others tossing trash from their lunch bags on the grass, and the wind carrying the litter into the river; he saw sewage from the community pumping station streaming out of a pipe into another creek, and he saw men in a boat yard spill gasoline into the river while they were filling their tank. He saw these things and the great buffalo took him over another part of the river where thousands of fish lay dead on the top of the water. And Peter became sad.

"We did that! We killed the fish and everything else because we didn't care what we did with our trash, chemicals, fertilizer or sewage. The fish were like the buffalo you showed me—they died and people helped kill them and I feel bad. But what can I do, what can I do. .?"

Suddenly, the dream ended. As Peter opened his eyes he was looking into the old Indian's face. The carved buffalo was in his hand.

"You're okay now Peter. You're okay," the old man said. "We had quite a time but everything will be fine now. You are in my cottage and your parents will be here to get you soon."

"But what about the giant buffalo? What about all the dead fish and crabs and oysters? What about the buffalo that were shot on the plains?" Peter asked excitedly.

"Peter, it is time for rest now. When you fell from the boat, you passed out. You were unconscious. Your buffalo is in your hand. You were dreaming and your dream vision was meant for you. It is the reason I gave you the gift of the buffalo."

"You want to use the water with your new boat. You want to watch the fishermen going out to collect their harvests. You want to enjoy what the Bay and what the big river can give you. But you cannot have these things if the waters are not healthy and the wildlife and river creatures disappear like the buffalo of the Great Plains."

"Why can't we do what the conservationists did for the buffalo and rockfish? Why can't we do those things for the other animals, fish and plants in the river? We could stop seeing things die in the river and see them live better," Peter said.

"We can do it and that is what you must do. And all your young friends and their mothers, fathers, sisters, brothers...everyone must work to make the water healthy so that the plants, animals and water creatures do not leave us forever," the old man said.

"Okay so what can we do?" asked Peter

"Start today," responded the old Indian. "Learn all that you can learn about our waters and what is wrong with them. Ask your father and mother to tell the school and government leaders that they want healthy water for the children. Find out from the conservation groups what you and your friends can do to help the water. Things like picking up trash and litter, not wasting precious water, and not washing your father's truck or your boat with poisonous soap which goes into the river where young crabs and fish are trying to grow. There are many things you and your friends can learn and that you can do from now on until you are an old man like me."

"But first and most important" the old man said, "is to remember your buffalo and always teach people that unless everyone helps to save our great waters, the creatures will disappear as the buffalo from the Great Plains. And, like the Indians who depended on the buffalo, you too will be sad.

"We both need rest now," he said. "You think about these things the buffalo and the river. Perhaps you will be the one person who makes the difference between a healthy river and one that is sad and sick."

"Thank you," Peter said while holding the wooden buffalo gently in his small hands. "I will never forget your words or my dream and I will work, no matter what else I do, to spend some of my time each day to help clean the environment, and also think about the buffalo."

A little while later, when Peter got up to meet his parents, the old Indian was peacefully staring out over the river, his hands folded in his lap, rocking slowly in his chair. And as Peter walked out of sight around the corner of the cottage he heard the old man softly say, "You are welcome anytime to tell me what is happening to save the waters. Good-bye."

Did You Know You Can Help In Many Ways, Every Day, To Help Save Our Rivers?

WATER

There are many things you can do to conserve water and break harmful water-use habits. Changing your habits can actually aid the Bay and rivers by reducing the amount of water that must be treated by sewage treatment plants. Less water to treat means the treatment plants will work more efficiently.

YOU CAN:

_____ Take shorter showers and shower less often.

_____ Turn off the water while brushing your teeth, soaping hands, washing and rinsing the dishes.

_____ Suggest to your parents and friends that they practice water saving techniques by helping to:

Install low flow showerheads to save water.
Fix a leaky faucet quickly.
Wash clothes and dishes only when there is a full load.
Collect rain water for your lawn and garden.

YARD AND GARDEN

Many pesticides are harmful to aquatic and terrestrial life. Fertilizers can wash off or move through the soil and cause over-nutrification of local water bodies and the Bay.

YOU CAN:

_____ Tell your parents to stop using herbicides and insecticides. Be careful not to over-fertilize. Apply fertilizers based on soil needs and product instructions.

_____ Choose plants for your yard that won't need pesticides or fertilizers.

_____ Contact the National Wildlife Federation about participating in their Backyard Wildlife Habitat Program, Dept. MO, 1400 16th Street, NW, Washington, DC 20036-2266.

WASTE DISPOSAL

The entire nation is facing a solid waste problem. We are creating so much trash that we cannot handle it all. Landfills are closing because they are full or contaminating groundwater, a common source of drinking water.

YOU CAN

_____ Separate garbage into paper, cans, glass, trash for recycling.

_____ Be aware of waste disposal problems and reduce the amount of solid waste you produce.

_____ Buy items packaged in biodegradable and/or recycled containers or buy recyclable materials.

_____ Re-use materials, such as paper bags, and wash materials such as aluminum foil, plastic bags, plastic cups, bowls, silverware, etc. to reuse instead of discarding them.

_____ Pick up litter, even if you did not put it there. (Litter can eventually wind up in the Bay or in your local stream.) Have a school or neighborhood clean-up day to clean public areas including beaches, bus stops, etc.

_____ Cut up plastic ''six-pack'' holders before throwing them away.

EROSION

Soil that washes away from bare spots in your yard or schoolyard can enter streams and the Bay and choke aquatic life, block sunshine, and carry unwanted nutrient. Controlling this type of erosion and run off on property and in your community will benefit air quality.

YOU CAN:

_____ Plant bare areas with grass or ground cover, or better yet with trees and shrubs. (These plantings improve wildlife habitat, attratcting birds and mammals to your home.)

_____ Start a program in your school or neighborhood to plant vegetation on bare areas.

STREAMS

Stream health is important to aquatic life. If you live near a stream or river you can enhance wildlife habitats and help ensure the survival of many animals.

YOU CAN:

_____ Help monitor the health of a local stream, perhaps even join a group such as Save Our Streams.

_____ Clean up trash and debris from streams and shorelines.

_____ Remove fish barriers such as junk cars, tires, appliances, etc. from streams so that fish can easily get upstream to spawn.

_____ Enhance habitat by building nest boxes for ducks.

ENERGY

You can help conserve energy. This will help the Bay because power generation facilities can hurt water quality. Mine drainage, oil spills, and oil refinement can harm aquatic life.

YOU CAN:

_____ Turn off electrical items when not in use.

_____ Ride a bicycle or walk instead of using a car.

_____ Keep your house cooler in the winter and warmer in the summer to save energy.

TOXICS

Many common household and automotive products are toxic. Harmful substances in these products often find their way into the water supply through septic systems and sewer lines which are not designed to filter out these chemical wastes.

YOU CAN:

_____ Learn about "household toxic wastes" and be aware of how to dispose of them.

_____ Stop pouring toxic substances (solvents, paints, preservatives, etc.) down drains or toilets.

_____ Stop dumping wastes or even leaves and trash down storm drains.

Other Books By Mick Blackistone

The Day They Left The Bay: An exciting children's story about environmental education, with illustrations by Lee Boynton. Winner of the U.S. Environmental Protection Agency Environmental Education Achievement Award, 1989. Ages 6 and up.   Retail $14.95

Just Passing Through: A beautiful book of insightful poetry with photographs by renown photographer Marion Warren.   Retail $13.95

Sun Up To Sundown: Watermen of the Chesapeake: An informative documentary with photographs by James Parker, of the changing lives for men who work the water. In their own words the commercial watermen discuss their way of life and what is affecting them in the 90's.   Retail $19.95

To order first edition signed copies: Send check or money order to:
Blue Crab Press, 3 Church Circle, Suite 140, Annapolis, MD 21401
or call
301-263-8490
Maryland residents include 5% sales tax.

The Day They Left The Bay: _____ signed copies at $14.95 each _____ plus tax.

The Buffalo And The River: _____ signed copies at $14.95 each _____ plus tax.

Just Passing Through: _____ signed copies at $13.95 each _____ plus tax.

Sun Up to Sundown: Watermen Of The Chesapeake: _____ signed copies at $19.95 each _____ plus tax.

_____ tax (Md. residents)

$3.00 shipping

_____ Total enclosed

For book signings and discount price-list for quantity orders to stores, schools, museums, etc., call 301-263-8490 for further information.